VANISHING
TRICK

For John, Fred and Leo
and my mother, Vivien Asquith

*and special thanks to Cheryl Moskowitz,
Helen Mackintosh, Polly Pattullo
and Rachel Hodgkin*

JANETTA OTTER-BARRY BOOKS

Text and illustrations copyright © Ros Asquith 2015
The right of Ros Asquith to be identified as the author and
illustrator of this work has been asserted by her in
accordance with the Copyright, Designs and Patents Act,
1988 (United Kingdom).

First published in Great Britain and in the USA in 2015 by
Frances Lincoln Children's Books,
74-77 White Lion Street, London N1 9PF
www.franceslincoln.com

A catalogue record for this book is available
from the British Library.

ISBN 978-1-84780-539-3

Printed and bound by CPI Group (UK) Ltd, Croydon, CR0 4YY

9 8 7 6 5 4 3 2 1

VANISHING TRICK

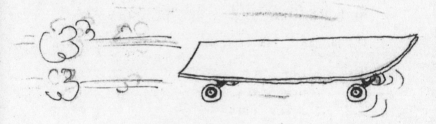

Poems by
Ros Asquith

Frances Lincoln
Children's Books

Contents

Line

I thought I would drop you a line.
Look, it's not very hard to define.
It's thin and it's dark, a discreet enough mark,
You can see its potential in mine ⎯⎯⎯⎯

Now that I've dropped you a line
You may do with it just as you please.
You may, if you wish, employ it to fish
Or to set up a tightrope for fleas.

You may choose to stretch it from here to there
Or to coil it up tight like a spring.
You may choose to knot it or whirl a lasso,
Or to loop it up into a swing.

You may want to write me a letter
Or draw ANYTHING nice with your line.
For this line makes a tree, a circle, a bee.
Oh, how I wish it were mine!

But this line is yours now forever ⎯⎯⎯⎯
It's as long as you want it to be.
Take it or leave it, thread it or weave it,
It's a line of poetry.

My Mind

In my head's a journey that only I can take,
there is no one else can ever read my mind.
I must tread carefully, for all the thoughts I make
must be mine alone, not lost upon the wind.

Inside are paths and mazes.
There are caverns, pits and keys.
There are wolves and saints and crazes.
A wave, a storm, a breeze.

There are patterns, wonder, colours.
Music, thunder, voices.
My mind is like no other's –
Only I can make my choices.

Mind out, that is, if you don't mind,
I must be gentle, treat it kind.
Your mind is your own, I think you'll find.
One day I hope to know my own mind.

DYSLEXIaaAAAARGH

Words are hard,
I don't mean talking
I don't mean chats,
I mean when words are walking
All over the page.
Then they're hard
they're bats
I'm in a rage.

Letters are mad things
they swirl about
daft as brushes
in and out
they won't stay in the book
they stops, then they rushes
there goes one! Look!
I'm thinking carefully how
I might just catch an 'a'
I think I've seen one now –
But zaaaaaaap. It flew AwAy.

I'm going to creep up sneakily
Now watch, as I lasso a 'b'
MayBe if I tread carefully
I can make it Be friends with me.

But it's gone, see?
It's gone all hazy
into a 'd'
No NO NO I'm not lazy.
It isn't me
The ALpHaBEt is crazy.

It needs to be locked up
all of it, yeh, all twenty six
letters, to stop their tricks.
Catch them now! Do it quick!
Before they all split.

Lock them up and chain them
knock them down and brain them
tame them and restrain them
put them in a border
put them all in order
they make me sick.

My teacher's sighing
my mum's crying
I ain't lying
I *am* trying.

But I'm about done with reading
I don't think it's reading I'm needing.
It's racing and chasing
and rushing and swirling
and gushing and whirling.
And circling and soaring
and floating and roaring.
Just like letters.
But better.

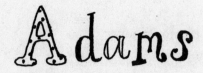Adams

There's three Adams in Mrs Turner's class,
Adam B, Adam W, Adam T,
and three Adams in my class,
Adam F, Adam R, Adam D.

Adam B is sporty,
Adam W is good at sums,
Adam T is naughty,
Adam F's got double-jointed thumbs.
Adam R can wiggle his ears.
But Adam D never comes.

Miss Pole does the register.
'Where is Adam D?
Has anybody seen him?
Wherever can he be?

We've written to his mother,
We've written to his dad,
We've even asked his brother.
It's really very sad.

We've tried hard to discover
why he will not come,
but his parents and his brother
say that he's struck dumb.

Can YOU find out, Evelyn?
He's very fond of you.
Just pop round after school, please,
and try to ask him, do.'

So I went round to Adam D's.
He lay upon his bed.
'Why don't you come to school no more?'
And this is what he said.

'Too many Adams.'

Well, would you Adam and Eve it?

'Adam and Eve it' is Cockney
rhyming slang for 'believe it'.

Jane Lee

Little Jane Lee
climbed a tree,
said, 'It's here I want to be.'
Mrs Lee said, 'Goodness me,
come down from that scary tree!'

'I was down before, I was feeling quite down,
now I'm high in clouds with a view of the town.
I think I'll stay, for I do believe
I like it here, up among the leaves.'

'Stuff and nonsense,' said Mrs Lee.
'You'll be down in no time, just you see.'

But no time passed and still Jane Lee
perched on the branch of the old oak tree.

She'd nuts from squirrels, crumbs from birds.
Not long before she lost human words.
Not long before, in the coldest weather,
she felt an itch – and grew a feather.
A sparrow's first, then a robin's, a crow's
and fine eagle feathers in golden rows.

Listen to Jane Lee! Hear how she sings!
And people are saying that she's grown wings.

'Where's Jane?' asked her sister, and Mrs Lee
said, 'Away with the fairies if you ask me.'
Or, 'She's joined the angels,' (which grown-ups say
when people die, or 'pass away').

But you and I know that little Jane Lee
sings, and flies, and sleeps in a tree.

Anthony's hair

Anthony Carstairs has got no hair.
He said he'd lost it so I said, 'Where?
Where was the last place you saw it?' I said.
'That's where you should look.'
 And he said, 'My head.'

(It isn't like losing your socks or key.
Everyone knew all about it but me.)

Later Miss told me that Anthony's ill
so his hair's fallen out and he's thin.
He's taking treatment, a shed-load of pills
and he's battling and certain to win.

(I had missed the first week of term, you see,
so everyone knew about it but me.)

'Not battling,' said Anthony, down by the square.
'Not battling, just getting by.
But I hate being bald when all of you stare.'
But Anthony didn't cry.

Next day, woolly hat, pulled over his ears.
'That's cool,' I said. 'No, it's hot.'
So I had an idea and I texted our year.
Not just my class, I texted the lot.

We all wore woolly hats to school
And Miss looked at us in despair.
'Hats off in class, you know the rules.'
And none of us had any hair.

(We'd all of us shaved our heads, you see,
we hoped it would help our Anthony.)

Miss said that she that was proud of us,
but Anthony looked at the floor.
He's not a boy who likes a fuss.
I wish I had thought some more.

It isn't like losing your socks or key.

Jo's House

My brother was just ten and I was eight.
We travelled on the coffee-coloured bus
which stopped outside Jo's coffee-coloured gate.
Our holiday – just Nan and Jo and us.

We raced, hens scattering, up the gravel path,
Jo's familiar greeting, arms thrown wide.
'How well you look,' she always welcomed us.
You never would have guessed that Jo was blind.

Jo's wallpaper was flock, her carpet brown,
her radio the size of two TVs.
Her house, her street, her little seaside town
safe harbour where we did just as we pleased.

Each Easter we hid eggs on top of shelves.
Jo's feeling fingers found each one all right.
'These eggs – have they been laid by magic elves?'
You never would have guessed she had no sight.

Was Jo not sad to only hear and feel?
When I was ten I asked her, did she mind?
She said her searching self made all things real.
She said, 'I never think that I am blind.'

She said inside her head the world burned bright.
She said, 'Inside my mouth bursts sour and sweet.
My ears can hear the birds as they take flight.
I feel the turning Earth beneath my feet.'

She said, 'I smell the toast if it is burning,
and when I seek, you know I always find.
I understand you may believe I'm yearning.
I'm not – I never think that I am blind.'

She saw my childhood soul, did Jo,
and knew all that there was to know.

KISSES

Each night, before I go to sleep,
I kiss my pictures twice.
I kiss eight horses
(that's sixteen).
I kiss my dead nan, my dead gran,
my dead mum
(that's six).
I kiss my old house (two).
I kiss Justin Bieber (two).
I kiss Lady Gaga (two).
That's 28 kisses.

But I'm growing out of Justin Bieber
so that'll soon make it 26.
Which is still a whole lot of kisses
that no one really feels.
I'm wondering, could I? Should I?
Kiss somebody real?

DiFFeRenT

I want to be wild as a caged bird.
I want to be dark as the light.
I must sing like a fish, I must weep like a stone.
I want to be bright as the night.

I want to be heavy as feathers
And to float on the ocean like lead.
To be quiet as thunder and fierce as a lamb
And never to sleep in a bed.

I want to run faster than lamp posts.
I want to be dry, like the sea.
To fly like a flower, to flame like the ice.
I want to be free to be me.

A dream of God

I dreamed of a being who held me in his hand,
who loved me, who understood.
Who looked like no being from any earthly land.
Still I knew that He was God.

'Do you believe in Him?' I asked the gentle cow.
'I do,' she mooed, 'for He is wise.
He causes calves to grow, milk of kindness to flow.
He is the Great Bull of the skies.'

'Do you believe in Him?' I asked the butterfly.
'Of course I do, else tell me who
turns a caterpillar to such a one as I,
except Lord Butterfly on high?'

'Do you believe in Him?' I asked
    the Ancient Greek.
'Him, possibly, but many more –
such wondrous gods, my child, who
    every language speak.
Apollo, Zeus, Diana, Thor.'

'Do you believe in Him?' I asked my kitchen table
(I know that tables cannot talk).
Yet my dream table was certainly most able:
'If these legs of mine could walk
I'd show you the great forest that held the tall tree,
the pine tree from whence I came.
The carpenter who felled it and from it fashioned me
is my God,
though I know not his name.'

Is there a God for each of us?
All creatures great and small?
For household things? For plants? For stones?
And a God of nothing at all?

BLACK & White

My friend's dog is black and white
Coal black spots on snowy fur.
I like Pongo.

My mum's newspaper is black and white
You can make boats and hats with it.
I like paper boats (but they sink).

My dad's puzzles are black and white
They're hard to do.
My dad loves crosswords (but I don't).

Our kitchen floor is black and white
And great for sliding on.
I'm crazy about floor skating.

My family is black and white
My dad is black and my mum is white.
I love my family.

But, really, my dad is dark brown, like a tree trunk
And my mum is pinky beige, like a party biscuit
And my brother is dark gold, like toffee
And I'm deep tan, like fudge.

And my auntie Nell is pale gold, like cream
And my auntie Vera is deep brown, like a bear
And my uncle Conrad is dark red, like a beetroot
And my uncle Ivan is rich mahogany,
     like a wardrobe
And my grandpa Sid is hot red, like a carrot
And my grandpa Jonah is cool hazel,
     like a skipping rope
And my grandma Augusta is warm red,
     like a chestnut

And my grandma Evy is shiny sable,
    like a magician's wand.
And my great great auntie Esmerelda is
    lightest grey, like smoke
And my great great uncle Zebedee is
    pale yellow, like a lemon
And my cousins on one side are every kind of
    dusky dark, from coffee to walnut to ebony
And my cousins on the other side are every kind
    of washy pale, from milk to rose to sand.

So are we a rainbow, or what?

? Question ?

If we had everything we want –
the music, toys, the food,
perfect schools, perfect dads,
all things easy and good.
And none of the things we don't want –
no worries, anguish, fuss.
No mad days, bad days, sad days –
would we still be us?

SANS SERIF

She pirouettes by, on silvery points
VICTORIA, VICTORIA, VICTORIA CONDENSED
her breath with sweetness all anoints
VICTORIA, Victorious, VICTORIA CONDENSED.

Her hair a stream of burnished gold.
And here am I, **Bodoni Bold**.

Smart alec, smart *italic Gill*
has calm Helvetica in tow
I'm getting smaller, feeling ill
feeling squeamish, feeling low.

Helvetica's point size 8, I'm told.
And me? I'm just **Bodoni Bold**.

Here's Times, sedate and in control
with Palatino at his side
serifs shining as they stroll
along the vellum smooth and wide.

I'm crouching, tucked behind a fold.
I know my place: **Bodoni Bold**.

Now **Techno** comes, relaxed and cool
roller-blading down the page
Verdana skates the inky pool
glistening; I feel my age.

Is it that I'm tired, or old?
Or just that I'm **Bodoni Bold**?

Elegant, eloquent, all of a type
on paper and package and screen
all full of character, all full of hype
all need to be read, to be seen.

And me? I'm left to gather mould
because I'm plain **Bodoni Bold**.

No one likes my type. But why?
Perhaps
I'm too **Bodoni** Shy?

*All these names are the real names
of different kinds of typefaces.*

READING

I've just read *Northern Lights*,
my soul is hurting.
My father's a vicar.
Am I deserting?

I'm wired, inspired,
astonished, sad.
My heart's on fire,
wounded but glad.

I'm on an ice floe
with Lyra there,
and the shield of a great white
armoured bear.

Once reading was so gentle.
PEEPO, Dogger,
I loved those books
and I love them still.

I revisit *Mother Hubbard,*
The Indian in the Cupboard,
James and the Giant Peach
whenever I'm ill.

But now my life is a new book opening,
mixing sunshine with shadows, fears with joy.
It's exciting but scary to learn what a man is,
I hope I can learn it and still be a boy.

Mohammed & the WHALE

Mohammed, of number 42
Cranmore Gardens, outside Crewe,
had a wish he knew would make him glad,
and every night he told his dad:
'Dad, I've GOT to learn to sail.'
'Why?' 'I've GOT to meet a whale.'
'Of course you have,' his father said.
'Now clean your teeth and off to bed.'

Mohammed, of number 42
Cranmore Gardens, outside Crewe,
had a dream he felt was surely true
and from Dad to Mum he brightly flew.
'Mum, I've GOT to learn to sail.'
'Why?' 'I've GOT to meet a whale.'
'Of course you have,' his mum replied.
'But it's getting late, run on inside.'

No matter how much he begged and cried
his only wish was thus denied.
But his dreams were filled with the wild commotion
of singing whales in a restless ocean.

Mohammed, of number 42
saved and saved till his money grew,
and took a train right down to the sea.
Out all alone at night – he was free!
He sneaked on a liner and hid in a crate
and biscuits and water were all that he ate.
Till he crept on deck one misty morning
to scan the horizon, sleepily yawning.

And he gazed and gazed with his sleep-filled eyes
at the line where the oceans meet the skies.
Till he saw a shimmer, a flick of a tail
and a plume of spray. A whale. A whale!

Mohammed, of number 42
Cranmore Gardens, outside Crewe,
knew exactly what he had to do.
So he lowered a lifeboat and in he jumped
and over the waves he hurtled and bumped.
How the boat rocked! How his heart thumped!

The great waves crashed and the wild wind roared.
He gazed at the creature he so adored,
The great blue whale, his friend-to-be,
his hero, his longed-for giant of the sea.

Until he was near as near could be.
Alone in the ocean, the whale and he.

'Whale,' thought Mohammed.
The whale thought, 'Boy.'
And Mohammed rose up on a wave of joy.
Stretched, and leapt, and grasped the tail
as you must, if ever you meet a whale.
Whale sped off across the foam
fierce and free in his ocean home.
Whale and boy in clouds of spray
plunging and swimming the live-long day.

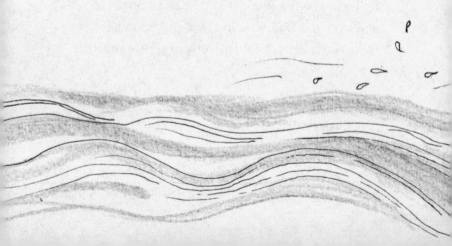

Night fell
and Mohammed decided to stay.
To play with the whale.
And play. And play.

So if ever you happen to see a whale
with a slim boy flying along on his tail,
that'll be Mohammed, of 42
Cranmore Gardens, outside Crewe.

Limerick Lick

There was a young person from Limerick
who wanted to be in a limerick.
She stayed up all night
but try as she might
she could not find a good rhyme for Limerick.

(Which is a shame, because she might
have used a candle with a
trimmer wick,
or
become a better
swimmer, quick,
or
learnt to sing a
hymn, or nick
a fortune from a
dimmer Rick,
or
even pulled a
grimmer trick
and delivered to poor
Jim or Mick

or Slim, a kick
or
even flung at
him a brick
or
made him shiver,
shimmer: sick.
Or,
if feeling
primmer, stick
to just the town of
Limerick.)

Solo

Noah was big,
Noah was proud,
his belly broad,
his bellow loud.
He and his sons
worked night and day,
pausing now and then to pray
and glance at each passing cloud.

The ark grew tall,
the ark grew long.
Its prow was sharp,
its keel was strong.
While I stood by on the hill alone,
my hooves embedded in mud and stone,
knowing I didn't belong.

The rains began
to trickle down.
The water rose
around the town.
And I stood by alone on the hill
and I longed to join (and I long to still)
as Noah gazed up to frown.

'You cannot come.
I am sorry for you,
but you are one
and we must have two.
It matters not how great your need.
We must take pairs, for pairs will breed.'
I ask you, what could I do?

So I stood and I watched,
with my head held high,
as the water rose
over wheat and rye,
and the animals went in pair by pair.
And I longed and longed to join them there.
But all alone was I.

I stood and I stared
as they sailed away,
as the water rose
to drown the day,
till I took to the sky,
where still I fly,
where on silvery nights you may
    hear me neigh.

Yes, at night you may see me,
a gleam in the dark,
swooping low
over street and park.
The one winged horse, since time began,
rejected both by God and Man.
Forever left out of the ark.

TALKING DOWN

When I was six I was dancing
And a grown-up said to me,
'Do you want to be a dancer?
Is that what you will be?'

'I am a dancer,' I said to him.
'It's very plain to see.
I'm dancing, therefore I'm a dancer.
So what do you mean, *will be?*'

Who's Counting?

One stake
Two fangs
Three coffins
Four castles
Five juicy necks.

Who's counting?
Count Dracula.
Obviously.

Innerdreamagain

Little crazy raindrop running down the pane,
trying to catch up with all the other rain.
Little slinky raindrop
wanting to be free
just like me.
'Dan, are you in a dream again?'

Used to be a time, can't remember when,
I felt like other kids, but that was then.
Seems so long ago
Seems so long ago
Seems so long ago
before the Bad Thing.
'Dan, are you in a dream again?'

If I could, I would explain
the cause of all this pain.
Trouble is,
I just can't remember.
I try to work it out
But my life is one long shout.
'DAN! Are you in a dream AGAIN?'

Doggerel

I'm going to teach
my dog to talk.
What'll he say?
'Time for a walk.'

The GORGON speaks

His hair was golden cherries
His lips were crimson berries
He was the best thing to happen all day.
All my life, really. 'Please stay.'
I warned him, 'Don't look me in the eye.'
And he, poor fool, said, 'Why?'

His hair is now stone cherries.
His lips are now stone berries.
He'd be better off in a vault.
I can't help it. It's not my fault.

SAT-IN HAT

I've got a new hat made of satin.
It's handy for keeping the cat in.
When people ask why
I reply with a sigh –

I like it much more than the hat before,
You know, the one that nobody wore,
A hat I admit she did adore
Until the day that she hurt her paw,
And kept meowing, it was so sore
(I think she caught it in the door).
You could see her bones. The blood! The gore!
And poor dear thing, she lost a claw!
You'd think she'd been in a cats' world war.
She aged overnight, she's only four –
We'd run out of medicine – I had to get more,
I spilled it all over the kitchen floor.
Clearing it up was a terrible chore.

Sorry, am I being a bore?

When people ask why,
I reply with a sigh –
There's blood on the old hat she sat in.

GEOMETRY

Ann Gull was **a cute** girl
though sometimes
o bleak day
she would get into a **right tangle.**

Sir Cumference tended to **circle**
O, O, O, round and round he'd go.
Hi**s fears**? He might get dizzy
(or lose his **compass**).

Ray Dius connected them, symmetrically.
He was **radiant**.

Shell Salesgirl

She sells sea shells by the sea shore.
She got fed up. 'Oh, such a bore.
I want to go to town
in a lavish golden gown,
not to be beside the seaside any more.
I want to go to the theatre –
I know there's something better
than selling stupid shells by the sad sea shore.
The sea shore makes me sick. It
makes me want to scream.'
So she upped and bought a ticket
to somewhere she could dream.

Left her mum a note: **Taking a train.**
Never, ever, coming home again.

Came to town, best thing yet.
Saw a sign: *Rooms to Let.*

She beheld three bells by a wee door.
Rang One, no fun. 'Oh, such a bore.
Horrid little room, vile little bed,
NO sea view.' Try Bell Two instead.
Rang Bell Two. Nothing new.
Rang Bell Three. Lost the key.
Slept on street. Got cold feet.
Texted Mum,
I've been dumb.
Can I come home? I miss the Sea.
Can I sell shells again? Love, Me.
You won't be surprised by what happened next.
Tears were shed, a flurry of texts.

Now she sells sea shells by the sea shore.

DRAGON

Life is dull for a dragon.
For a dragon, time drags on.
Frighten kid, eat princess,
breathe fire, cause distress.

Day after deadly day, the same.
Eat, scare, sleep, flame.

Hedgehog

Twilight in the garden
I can hardly see,
found a little hedgehog
underneath the tree.
Found a little hedgehog
oh so still.
Quiet little hedgehog
must be ill.
Made it a plate of milk and bread,
Put the plate down beside its head.
Quiet little hedgehog
IS that its head?
Did I put the food by its tail instead?

Made another plate of food
just in case.
Put it on the other side
(maybe that's its face).
Poor little hedgehog doesn't make a sound.
Quiet little hedgehog prone upon the ground.
But wait, this hedgehog's almost round!

I could've placed those plates
by its *sides*.
And it's too weak to move
if it tried!

I make a couple more
plates of milk and bread,
a plate at all four sides.
(One *must* be its head.)
It's pitch dark now
so I go to bed.

First thing next morning I wake in a worry.
Is my hedgehog living?
I'm outside in a flurry.

Plates are there, under the tree
where my hedgehog might still be.
But in the light of daytime
there's a sight to make me blush.
Circled by four plates of food
lies my spiky old hairbrush.

"Please, Miss"

I have had my hand up now
for 102 days, six hours, 48 minutes and
   17 seconds.
A hawk has built a nest in my hand
and laid six eggs.
504 flies have sat on my hand,
83 spiders,
4,792 microbes.
Air breathed by Jesus, Shakespeare,
   Buddha, Mohammed,
Pythagorus, Atilla the Hun, Eddie Izzard and
Enid Blyton has circulated around it.
Miss never picks me,
even when I say 'Please, Miss',
and even though I have had my hand up now
for 102 days, six hours, 48 minutes and
   47 seconds
(or however long it has taken you to read this).
The eggs are about to hatch.
Soon there will be baby hawks swooping around,
pecking our eyes and pooing on our algebra.
'Yes, Sam, what is it?'
'Please, Miss, why do you never pick me?'

VOWEL MOVEMENTS

Today we are having a spilling test.
Please spill your words carefully.

Tomorrow I will ask you to odd up,
because tomorrow is moths.

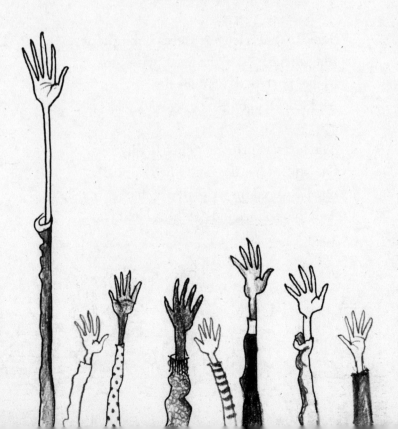

reedy MABEL

Sue had a greedy cat called Mabel
Who ate as much as she was able.
She ate jam tart, she ate pork pie
Till people said, 'She's sure to die.'

Then came the day, Sue's birthday feast.
Her father made a cake with yeast,
Eggs, butter, flour, raisins – the lot,
All baked in an enormous pot.

Some of Sue's friends were coming to tea,
But when she saw the feast, with glee
Mabel purred, 'It's all for me!'
And leaped upon that gorgeous tea.

The furry whirlwind gobbled jelly.
She stuffed her face and filled her belly.
She hoovered up six plates of ham
And fourteen rounds of bread and jam.

She ate the biscuits, ate the pastry
(bless my paws but that was tasty).
She ate the crisps and all the sponge
And finished off the pink blancmange.

She scampered round and round the table.
Oh feline fiend, Oh Greedy Mabel!
And when at last she'd had enough
She filled herself with fizzy stuff.

Ginger beer and orange pop –
It seemed as though she'd never stop,
But go on growing ever bigger
Till she completely spoilt her figure.

And so it happened, all too soon,
She grew as big as a balloon,
And an explosion rent the hall.
There was no Mabel left at all.

Now learn this lesson, children, do.
That party food was meant for you.
So if you hear some scampering paws,
Bar the windows! Lock the doors!

BULLY

Let's make fun of stupid Lou
who can't even tie his laces,
who can't add two and two,
who never wins any races
and pulls all those ugly faces.

Let's have a go at Miss Pool,
who thinks learning should be 'such fun'.
Laughing stock of the school,
her frizzy old hair in a bun.
And her belly, it must weigh a ton.

Now let's attack Mr Fain,
the lousiest possible head.
Peep inside his brain,
and you'll see that he's lost the thread.
Forgotten. Every. Word. He's said.

Or why not make fun of me,
for being so pointlessly cruel?
You think I am happy
to be chief bully of our school?
Take me down a peg, you fool.

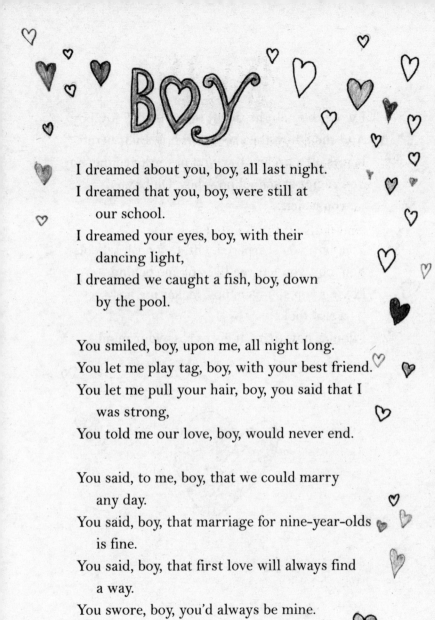

BOY

I dreamed about you, boy, all last night.
I dreamed that you, boy, were still at
    our school.
I dreamed your eyes, boy, with their
    dancing light,
I dreamed we caught a fish, boy, down
    by the pool.

You smiled, boy, upon me, all night long.
You let me play tag, boy, with your best friend.
You let me pull your hair, boy, you said that I
    was strong,
You told me our love, boy, would never end.

You said, to me, boy, that we could marry
    any day.
You said, boy, that marriage for nine-year-olds
    is fine.
You said, boy, that first love will always find
    a way.
You swore, boy, you'd always be mine.

I woke, boy, alight, adrift on clouds of joy, boy.
And then, boy, the shock. Oh boy, I felt bereft.
It was all a dream, boy, you never loved me, boy.
You're not at school now, boy. Oh boy,
    you've left.

You, boy, you scarpered. Off to a posh school.

You, boy, you left the likes of me behind.

Loving you so much, boy, makes me feel
    a real fool.
I doubt, boy, that I'll ever cross your mind.

*TRANSFORMATION

There's a shaggy old nag at the stables I clean.
His name is Socrates.
Got a scraggy old mane and scrofulous hooves
and broken old, scabby old knees.

When kids come for rides they abhor him.
'He looks like an understuffed sofa.
The best thing to do is ignore him,
he's a hopeless, pathetic old loafer.'
(But old Socrates – I adore him.)

I hear the riding instructor
whisper Socrates must go.
'Dog food is all he is good for,
none of the kids need know.'

So at night I creep into the stables I clean
and steal Socrates away.
And I take him up to the common
and I stuff him with oats and hay.

I clip his old mane, I groom his old coat,
I polish his old hooves to shine.
I bandage his knees and I beg him to, please,
just follow these words of mine:

'I will teach you to jump, you dear old lump.
I will teach you to canter and trot.
At the gentlest touch, it will not need much,
I will train you to dance on the spot.'

For days, weeks and months I school him
and Socrates starts to improve.
Was it only the food he needed?
Or was it, perhaps, the love?

I steal him back to the stables I clean,
tell them his name is Black Knight.
'He's the best pony ever,
his dressage is clever,
he jumps like a bird in flight.'

Now he's the most popular pony
and the riding instructor is pleased.
And I'll never tell of his secret:
that Black Knight is old Socrates.

AMAZE

I'm building a maze,
an amazing maze,
with traps and holes and snares.
To trip you up,
to swallow you whole,
to catch you unawares.

I'm making long tunnels,
a furnace with funnels,
the walls are studded with nails.
Rats infest the place,
they leap at your face.
My amazing maze never fails.

I'm building it high, I'm digging it long,
each turning you take will always be wrong.
Here's a poisonous claw, an invisible door,
electric eels all over the floor.
It's haunted just here,
there's a shark pond just there.
Boiling oil and quicksand everywhere.

Enter at your peril. If you dare!

Museum of the Future

Here is an ancient object
preserved from times long past.
Treat it, please, with some respect,
we hope that it will last.

You'll see it's coated now with fluff
and doesn't look like much.
It's made of very fragile stuff
called *paper*. Do not touch!

This thing's been here for ages
and has lost its former glory.
But see? These parts are *pages*
and this thing here's a *story*.

It may sound quite absurd, it's true,
but take a closer look.
This was once loved, I promise you.
Its name? They say it's *Book*.

STOP IT

'Stop it now!'
'How?'
'I don't care how,
just stop it now!'
'Stop what?'
'Stop your rot!'
'With what?'
'Try a full stop, my friend
and you'll come to the end,
try it now, here's how –'.

<u>Do</u>n't call me 'GINGER' (ever)

I love my freckles,
my chestnut speckles,
which come out like flowers in the sun.

I adore my red hair,
my halo, my flair.
But it seems I'm the only one.

I will wave my wand,
turn brunette and blonde
into a blazing red.

So you'll all agree
it's better to be
flaming scarlet instead.

Otherwise, why not admire
my blazing self, my head of fire?

girl next door

I kissed the girl who kissed the boy
Who kissed the girl next door.
Which means I've nearly kissed the girl
Who I am waiting for.

Our houses nest like mirrors,
Our rooms are feet apart.
Which means I've always slept beside
The girl who's won my heart.

She loved me in Year Three,
She despised me in Year Four.
But I feel she'll like me next year,
The girl I'm waiting for.

Alone

I want to be alone today,
I want to be alone.
I want to be alone, I say,
That means, be on my own.

I'm talking to myself today
(I really hope you'll keep away).
Sometimes it is the only way
to find just what I want to say.

I need to be alone.

Poetry Lesson

In the hour I met her for
she taught me about metaphor.
I said our smiles were similar,
she, smiling, showed me similes.
She sold me a sonnet.
I asked, 'What's on it?'
She talked about syllables
which weren't on her syllabus.

She valued blank verse,
she romanced about rhyme.
Best of all she taught me
how to beat time.

GRASS

Lying on the grass, falling into the sky,
pretending the grass is nine miles high.
I am smaller than a spider's eye.

A grain of sand is big as a planet.
My name's Ramona (instead of Janet).
I live in Peru (instead of Thanet).

Lying on the grass, falling into the sky.
Knowing I can fly.

Mr Jones (with apologies to Dr Fell)

I do not like you, Mr Jones.
You give me shivers in my bones.
I do not like your cold dead stare,
the way you try to touch my hair
(your hand that rasps, your eyes that glare).

Perhaps I am not being fair.
If so, I must say I don't care.
You give me shivers in my bones.
I do not like you, Mr Jones.

Big Piano

I stayed the night with Annie,
she's the music teacher's daughter.
They hadn't got no fizzy drinks
so all I had was water.

But in the front room, guess what I saw?
A big piano that filled the floor.

We didn't go to bed till ten
as Annie's mum was playing
(bassoon I think she said it was,
like herds of donkeys braying).

Annie turned music she called a *score*
and the big piano filled the floor.

The beds were full and so I slept
across two kitchen chairs.
The cat slept right on top of me
and covered me in hairs.

I lay awake, staring through the door
at the big piano which filled the floor.

I dreamed a meal of piccolos,
we drank from mandolins.
We'd drums and buttered trumpets,
pudding was violins. In tins.

It wasn't very comfy, yet I wanted more
    and more
of the house with the piano filling all
    the floor.

Encore!

Vamp Ire

Count Dracula and Countess Drac
Nearly had two heart attacks
The day they heard their daughter say:
'Parents! Take my plate away.
You know I'm never ever rude
But I cannot abide your food.'
This speech was bad enough, but then
She said, 'I'm vegetarian.'

Dracula raised his wings up high
To loop the loop in the darkening sky.
'Vegetarian! No child of mine
Will ever ever take that line!
A vampire simply can't survive
Unless it feasts on something live!'

The countess wept, the countess wailed,
'Dracky darling, we have failed.
We have reared a nightmare daughter
Refusing blood, demanding water.
I'll become a nervous wreck
If she spurns to bite a neck.'

They tried to tempt her first with fishes
(served in most exotic dishes).
They offered haddock, cod and trout
But she preferred a Brussels sprout.
They proffered pork, made rich beef stew.
'Oh, try a mouthful, Vera, do!'
But, however hard they tried,
Vera's fangs were satisfied
With carrots, pumpkin, fresh string beans,
Tureens of healthy juicy greens.

'She's eating spinach! What is worse,
She may try fruit – it is a curse!'
And so the vampires moaned and groaned
And groaned and moaned and moaned
    and groaned.

It seems to me that whatever you do
Can be wrong for your parents
    but right for you.

ROOM

There's a room I will not enter
Has a corner I don't care for
Darkness lingers round its skirting
What would I go there for?

There's a door I will not open
Rusting hinges, paintwork greasy
Press my ear to hear the rustling
Something shifting, dark, uneasy.

I peered once through the window
Moth beat frantic on its pane
Found my courage, entered, freed it
I will not go there again.

There's a room I do not go to
Don't ask me why I do not go
Or why the poor pale moth was frantic
Believe me, you don't want to know.

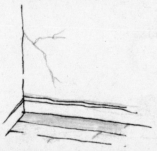

Things I Like

My fair hair
My arm charm
My wet pet
(he's a fish).

My dry eye
My pink drink
My best dress
(my wish).

My kind mind
My strong song
My grand
Handstand.

MisMaTch

She exploded tears, wore loud clothes,
Clashing florals, diamonds, swirls.
Her cacophony flailed his world,
His fragile ears, his inner flow.

Her noisy skin, her laughter whirring,
Even her eyes could scream.
He, flattened, tried to dream,
Shy as starlight, never stirring.

Her hair clattered, fingers snapped.
She hectoring, lecturing, wild,
He tiptoeing, whispering, mild.
Loud mother, quiet child: trapped.

Carthorse Orchestra

'Be nice to the new girl,
Her name is Anna.
Her name is Anna Gram.
Do you know what that means?'
'Yes, Miss, I do.'
'Excellent, please do tell us, Sam.'

'Well, it's kind of, you know,
don't know how to put it. . .'
'Why, then, Sam, did you put up your hand?'
'Well, it's when words, um,
have the same letters,
like *march* and *charm*.' 'Sam, that's grand.
Very good, excellent.
March and charm is excellent.
Can anyone think of other ones?'
'Me, Miss, I can,
I can think of hundreds.
Um, er, wait a sec, *snub* and *buns*.

And, you know, who's that
bloke in Star Wars?
Alec Guinness – he's *genuine class.*'

'Oh, that's lovely, so true, isn't it?
5P, you are my favourite class.'

We felt happy then.
It's nice when Miss Pole likes us.
She doesn't like us every day, that's for sure,
but we went home cheerful
instead of tearful.
We were all eager to find some more.

And the next day,
we had loads,
and three were quite tremendous.
Guess what *Charles Dickens* makes?
Wait for it: *children's cakes.*
I think that's stupendous.

Millenium Bridge
is *lemming builder.*
Wicked! But the best by far,
well, the one that I like best at least,
Is *carthorse* – and *orchestra.*

I imagine those grand musicians,
I imagine I hear them play.
The rows of giant horses
trotting in, carefully
lining up their instruments in golden hay.

A harness of harps
A bridle of bugles
A canter of cornets
A frolic of flugels
A trot of timpani
A buck of brass
A prance of piccolos
Deep bay of double bass

And here comes the soloist,
nostrils flared, eyes aflame,
pawing the ground, tossing his mane.
A great Shire stallion (in a medallion)
Music will never sound like this again.

I paint my carthorse orchestra.
I long to hear them play.
I listen to them in my dreams.
They've made my day.

WORD

When I hear the word *word*
My brain goes blurred
My mind feels furred.
Word is a strange word isn't it?
It has too many meanings, doesn't it?
After all, everything's a word.
How absurd.

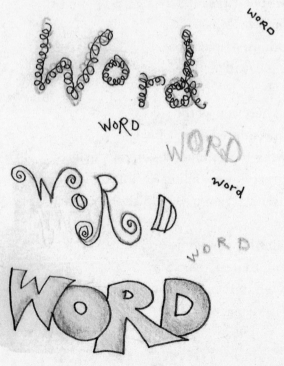

year six

Year Six Disco, playing spin-the-bottle
And it's not stopping at me
The girls have spun it to stop at Sam
22 out of 23!

So Sam got 22 kisses
And Mehmet and Billy got none
But the twenty-third kiss was the last
And that was the sweetest one.

The twenty-third kiss was from Anna
She stopped the bottle at me
Anna's the one with the laughing eyes
And Sam is as mad as can be.

S...L....O....W

'It's late, it's late. Brush your hair.'
But I'm watching a fly
climb up the stair.
Another few seconds and it'll be there.

'It's late, it's late. Where are your shoes?'
I've found one
but I'm not sure whose.
Why do they never stay in twos?

'It's late, it's late. Where's your folder?'
I'm ice-man,
freezing and getting colder.
So I can't move until I'm older.

'It's late, it's late. We'll miss the post.'
But I've got to nibble
this piece of toast
until it's exactly the shape of a ghost.

'It's late, it's late. We'll miss the shops.'
But I'm trying to count
how many hops
the sparrow does before it stops.

'It's late it's late. We'll miss them all.'
But I'm crawling along
a mile-high wall.
I'm Spiderman. D'you want me to fall?

'It's late, it's late. We'll miss the Fair.'
Coming, ready or not.

POMES

Miss says we got to bring in a pome.
Well I only know one pome.
'Diddle Diddle Dumpling my son John
went to bed with his trousers on.'
'You can't take that in,' says my mum.
'We don't want Miss to think you're dumb.
Get your skates on and we'll see
what they've got in the Library.'

So here we are and guess what's here?
A pome for each day of the year!
That's much more than we'll ever need.
It's going to take a year to read.

'I know,' I said, 'I'll get a pin
and flip the pages and stick it in.'
And do you know which pome I got?
It's by someone who's written an awful lot,
Who's written more pomes than all the rest
So I bet that I have chose the best.

I've read all of Anonymous's pomes now.
But I can't help thinking, all the same,
that if I was that good at writing poetry
I would definitely choose another name.

The JAY and the BEE

A B C A tree
but D B wants A flower.
D B say 'G
I need pollen power.'

E F no money
so D B need honey.

A J come flying
E C D B.
D J say 'come
N fly with me.'

'Y?' say D B
'I go high' say D J.
So D B N D J
fly away.

D B N D J fly for hours
D B N D J C some flowers.

D B, D J, U N I R happy, C.
Y? We have honey still for T.

Billy IS Batman

Billy is Batman.
He is, he really is!
I didn't believe it either at first.
But yesterday he showed me, he did,
   he really did.
He slid up his sleeve and he's got
Batman's Real Watch.
No, but it gets better.
It does, it really does!
On his belt he's got Batman's Grappling Hook.
Batman's Real Grappling Hook.
No, but serious, OK here's the best bit.
Under his fleece is Batman's Real Cloak.
There, you believe it now.
Ask him to show you.
Or you can ask Nat, cos Nat knows too.
Look, I promised
not to tell anyone,
but Nat is Robin. I swear it's true.

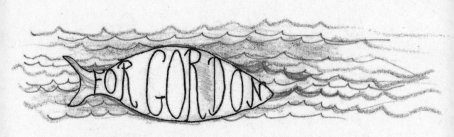

If I could have just one wish
I'd like a wish for my goldfish.
I did not care to see him die,
I could not see him in the sky
with goldfish angels floating by.
I could not see a goldfish god.
I tried, but it just seemed too odd.

What makes me sad as anything
is his life came to end
when all he'd done was swim about
and never had a friend.

So if I could have just one wish
I'd wish a friend for my goldfish.

What I go to school for

I don't like school
there's no use faking
I don't like school
I'd rather be taking
the ball to the park
or intrepidly wrestling
a humungous shark
or even doing something really boring
like counting the snorts while
    Granny's snoring.

But I go to school because
(don't tell anyone, no not anyone
don't tell anyone about this at all)
I go to school because
there's a girl there
a girl there
and I'm going to marry her
when I'm tall.

I have noticed her hair
how it curves on her cheek
I just sit and look at her
all through the week.

I have noticed her voice
though we never speak
I just like to listen to her
all through the week.

When we go up to Big School
she'll go to another
she's following after
her sister and brother.

So I'll have to propose before Year Six
and it's coming soon and I'm feeling sick.

Still, I've got a feeling she likes me too
And I'll wait for her
(but I won't go to school).

BOOK DAY

We've got Book Day next week,
I don't know what to do.
Have to dress up as a character
but I don't know who.

There'll be twenty Harry Potters,
a Mr Gum,
two Tracy Beakers,
a Tweedledum.

We've got Book Day in two days,
I don't know what to do.
Have to dress up as a character
but I don't know who.

There'll be some Horrid Henrys,
and a Winnie the Pooh,
thirty dirty witches,
a ghost or two.

We've got Book Day today.
'Mum, got spots. Look!
All right then, I'll tell you.
Supposed to dress up like a book.'

Mum sent me in anyway,
but it all turned out OK.
Guess what saved the day?
Half the school dressed up as books
and half the school didn't.
In my class, 14 did
and 16 didn't. Phew.

The Cherry Pie

One day while walking down the lane
I met a cherry pie.
'Hello,' I said.
It shook its head.
So, 'Cheerio,' said I.

But damply dripping from its crust
I noticed one small tear.
I took it home,
I warmed it up.
It soon was full of cheer.

'How are you now, dear Cherry Pie?'
I asked, after a while.
'Crisply crump,'
the pie replied
and smiled a grateful smile.

It looked so cheerful sitting there,
so sweet, so very nice,
that while it hummed
a song of thanks
I quietly cut a slice.

Now harken to me, cherry pies!
Walk not in lanes when you are glum.
Or if you must
then dry your crust,
else you'll be eaten – every crumb.

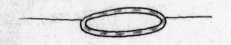

Boys don't CRY

If a girl falls over,
just a little fall,
something really small,
hardly hurt at all,
she weeps and wails and screams and cries
and everyone helps her dry her eyes.
'Oh dear, poor you, get a plaster,
come to Miss.'
And crowds of girls all stroke her hair and
give her knee a kiss.

But a boy can smash his head in
and all he gets is:
'All right, mate?'
If he's lucky.

Skateboard

My mum does not like my skateboard,
she thinks I'll come to harm.
Why does she always nag me?
All I did was break my arm.

This is she:
'I'll make it a hateboard
a confiscateboard
a you're-always-lateboard
a just-you-waitboard.'

This is me:
'I've got a dateboard
with my best mateboard
It's my open-the-gateboard
It's my first-rateboard'
I'm free. I'm fast.
I'm out at last.
I'm never ever ever bored
with my wonderful,
with my marvellous,
with my adored
skateboard.

SPORTS DAY

Egg and spoon, egg and spoon,
Line up for the egg and spoon.

No, Jordan, not prune and spoon.
No, Caroline, not balloon and spoon.
No, Donna, not humming a tune and spoon.
No, Michael, not jumping over the moon
    and spoon.

Egg and spoon, egg and spoon,
Egg and spoon race starting soon.

Now, children, listen, listen PLEASE.
Daryl, please get off your knees.
Gavin! Come down off those trees.
No. Egg and spoon. Not spoon and peas.
Stop scratching, Dan. Have you got fleas?
Or worse, some horrible disease?

Egg and spoon, egg and spoon,
Egg and spoon race starting soon.

Now, line up nicely, please don't run.
If you do you'll spoil the fun.

Walking quickly is the way,
I must insist on real fair play.
And *balance* the egg. I do mean you!
Give me that, you're using glue!
If I see anyone even so much
as giving their egg the slightest touch,
believe you me, you cannot hide.
You will be disqualified.
Stop it, Sarah, and give that back.
What is it? Goodness me, Blu Tack.

Egg and spoon, egg and spoon,
Egg and spoon race starting soon!

Sumil, you should be in a cradle,
that's not a spoon, it's a soup ladle.
And goodness me, what is that, Jade?
It's egg and spoon, not egg and spade.
And Mehmet, it's not quite the thing
to tie your egg with tape and string.
Well, I must say, that beats all –
Denzil's using a ping-pong ball.

Egg and spoon, egg and spoon,
Egg and spoon race starting soon.

On your marks, get set, GO.
Do NOT run! But don't be slow!
Egg and spoon, oh what fun.
The egg and spoon race has begun.

Seconds later, what a cheer.
Who's the winner? Over here!
He had Blu Tack, he had glue.
He never walked, he ran, he knew
that, for those who want to win,
cheating seems a minor sin.

But who's this coming last I see,
walking along so gingerly?
Holding her egg and head so high?
Is that a tear in her eye?
She didn't run, she didn't cheat.
But she surely, sorely, got dead beat.

No one else spots the lost look on her face.
They're working out how to win the next race.

Winter & Spring

The frost is white fire on the window pane,
The sun is pale fire in the sky,
The sky dazzles white around the sun.
They are waiting for you to come, my love,
Waiting till you come by.

For all the world's colour is in your heart,
In the golds and the blues and the green.
Yet when we meet we always must part
For our sweet love must never be seen.
I leave you the snowdrop, a token of love,
You leave me the evergreen.

At our brief meeting the difference is felt.
The whole land rejoices as my snows melt.
Who is to know that we love too much?
That the melting snows are my heart
    at your touch?
That the April showers are your sad tears?
I must run and you follow for infinite years.

STAYING

If I had a boat
I would float.
If I had a car
I'd go far.
In a plane or a train
I'd cross magic terrains,
Go thousands of miles to play.

But I am still small
And have nothing at all
So I grit my teeth and I stay.

Desdemona

Desdemona's big and pale
Desdemona's like a whale
She moves more slowly than a snail
Who's up to get Desdemona?

Desdemona's got no friends
Her hair's all stringy with splitty ends
When she wants to borrow, no one lends
Who's up to get Desdemona?

Desdemona never tries
Desdemona never cries
But sometimes you see her wipe her eyes
When she thinks no one's watching.

I thought about her all last night
Her big pale face all sad and white
I tried to shut my eyes up tight
To keep from seeing.

But I dreamed of her the whole night long
My heart tells me that it's all wrong
My head asks me if I feel strong
I cannot answer.

Vanishing Trick*

Amanda Jane's disappeared, you say?
It happens now and then.
It started when she was... I don't know,
can't quite remember when.

She might have been starting at Big School
with her brand new uniform on.
She'd sometimes turn pale
or you'd hear a wee wail
and FWOOF! Amanda'd be gone.

Or maybe when sitting at table
you'd ask her to eat up her ham.
She'd seem quite serene,
as calm as the queen,
when FWOOF! A spectacular scram.

And once I remember quite clearly
she asked for a room of her own.
'It must go to your brother,
there isn't another.'
But FWOOF! Away she'd flown.

Or the day she was watching the telly,
complaining her brain was all addled.
She came over dreamy
(the room felt quite steamy)
and FWOOF! She had skedaddled.

There was also a time when her uncle
tried to tickle her chin with his beard.
Well, she nodded and smiled
(she didn't seem riled)
Then FWOOF! She'd disappeared.

Now I understand this time it's different.
Suspected of murder, you say?
But she's such a dear,
she was sitting right here,
But FWOOF! She's vanished away.

Amanda Jane's been arrested?
Caught red-handed? Silly goose!
Killed her uncle? A knife?
Then she's sure to get life.
But FWOOF! (Hooray.) She's vamoosed.

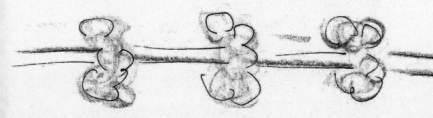

Mrs WORLD: a global Warning

Here's Mrs Volcano, vomiting ash, rumbling fire,
reciting a litany, Pompeii, Vesuvius, Montserrat.
Grrrrrrrrrrrrrrrrrrr.
Behind her Madam Desert, rippling, muscular,
her shifting sands dipping in search of oases.
Swisssssh.
And the great Queen Rainforest, shimmering, towering,
scattering luminous birds like loose change.
The earth trembles.
Hush.

The Empress Water speaks:
'Almost all we have is I
and every year that trickles by
yet another droplet seeps
deep into my darkest deeps.
Almost all we have is Me,
is river, ocean, lake and sea.
And yet I long and long to get
more and more, more wet, more wet.

And so I bid you, sisters all,
Sister Snowdrop, sweet and small,
Sister Ice-Cap, specially you,
here is all you have to do.
All your hopes have now gone west.
Why be bothered to protest?
Simply stand in line and wait,
drown your anger, slake your hate.

Instead, come make your peace with me,
come swim into my endless sea.
For you know you really oughta
be happy with your Sister Water.
Deserts will green beneath my waves
deep within these ocean caves.
Forests will be forever calm,
never more to suffer harm.
And even you, my Everest,
will sink into eternal rest.

For I can accommodate
humanity and all its hate.
Mankind will melt quite peacefully
deep within the sea of me.'

Best Mate

My lucky colour is blue
My lucky number is eight
My lucky toy is my catapult
My lucky friend is Fred Tate.

But I am happy with seven
And I am OK with red
And I can do without lucky toys
But I can't do without Fred.

Wishing Well

A wishing well
may seem swell.
But it feeds its fishes
on your wishes.
Oh well.

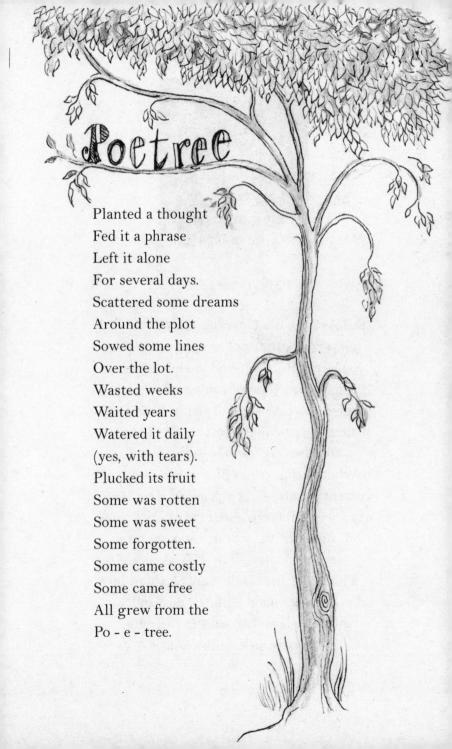

Poetree

Planted a thought
Fed it a phrase
Left it alone
For several days.
Scattered some dreams
Around the plot
Sowed some lines
Over the lot.
Wasted weeks
Waited years
Watered it daily
(yes, with tears).
Plucked its fruit
Some was rotten
Some was sweet
Some forgotten.
Some came costly
Some came free
All grew from the
Po - e - tree.

Ros Asquith is a Guardian Cartoonist and
author/illustrator of over 80 books for
young people, published in 18 languages.
She has painted murals in seven countries,
juggled in a circus, cuddled a wolf and was
theatre critic for *Time Out*, *City Limits*
and the *Observer*. She trained as a
psychodynamic counsellor at Birkbeck and
currently counsels at a primary school one
day a week. Ros answered only to the name
of Jim until she was five and has been
writing poetry since she was nine.
This is her first collection. She lives in
North London with her husband
and they have two sons in their 20s.
www.rosasquith.co.uk